M000248154

Flower Power
Hat, Scarf & Fingerless Gloves
DESIGNS BY **SUE CHILDRESS**

SKILL LEVEL

INTERMEDIATE

FINISHED SIZES
Doll: Fits 18-inch fashion doll
Child: Instructions given fit child's size small/medium; changes for child's size medium/large are in [ ].

FINISHED GARMENT MEASUREMENTS
Child's Hat: Approximately 19 [20] inches in circumference
Child's Scarf: 28 x 2 inches
Child's Fingerless Gloves: 6 inches in circumference x 3½ inches long
Doll's Scarf: 19 x 2 inches

MATERIALS
- Sport weight yarn: 350 yds periwinkle
- Size F/5/3.75mm crochet hook or size needed to obtain gauge
- Tapestry needle

2 FINE

GAUGE
9 hdc = 2 inches

Take time to check gauge.

PATTERN NOTES
Weave in ends as work progresses.

Join rounds with slip stitch as indicated unless otherwise stated.

Chain-3 at beginning of row or round counts as first double crochet unless otherwise stated.

Chain-2 at beginning of round counts as first half double crochet unless otherwise stated.

DOLL'S OUTFIT
HAT
BODY

Rnd 1 (RS): Ch 6, **join** (*see Pattern Notes*) in first ch to form a ring, **ch 3** (*see Pattern Notes*), 19 dc in ring, join in 3rd ch of beg ch-3. (*20 dc*)

Rnd 2: Ch 2 (*see Pattern Notes*), 2 dc in next dc, hdc in next dc, 2 sc in next dc, [hdc in next dc, 3 dc in next dc, hdc in next dc, 2 sc in next dc] around, join in 2nd ch of beg ch-2. (*34 sts*)

Rnd 3: Ch 1, sc in same ch as joining, [ch 3, sk next st, sc in next st] around to last st, ch 3, sk last st, join in first sc. (*17 ch-3 sps*)

Rnd 4: (Sl st, ch 2, 2 dc, hdc) in next ch-3 sp, (hdc, 2 dc, hdc) in each ch-3 sp around, join in 2nd ch of beg ch-2. (*68 sts*)

Rnd 5: Sl st in next dc, sc in natural sp before next dc, [ch 4, sk next 2 hdc, sc in natural sp between next 2 dc] around to last hdc, ch 4, sk last hdc, join in first sc. (*17 ch-4 sps*)

Rnd 6: (Sl st, ch 2, 2 dc, hdc) in next ch-4 sp, (hdc, 2 dc, hdc) in each ch-4 sp around, join in 2nd ch of beg ch-2. (*68 sts*)

Rnd 7: Ch 2, hdc in each st around, join in 2nd ch of beg ch-2.

Rnd 8: Ch 1, sc in same ch as joining, [ch 3, sk next 3 hdc, sc in next hdc] around to last 3 hdc, ch 3, sk last 3 hdc, join in first sc. (*17 ch-3 sps*)

Rnd 9: (Sl st, ch 3, dc, sc) in next ch-3 sp, (2 dc, sc) in each ch-3 sp around, join in 3rd ch of beg ch-3. (*51 sts*)

Rnd 10: Ch 1, sc in same ch as joining, [ch 3, sk next 2 sts, sc in next st] around to last 2 sts, ch 3, sk last 2 sts, join in first sc. (*17 ch-3 sps*)

Rnds 11 & 12: Rep rnds 9 and 10. At end of rnd 12, fasten off.

FLOWER

Rnd 1 (RS): Ch 6, join in first ch to form a ring, ch 3, 23 dc in ring, join in 3rd ch of beg ch-3. (*24 dc*)

Rnd 2: [Ch 5, sc around post of next dc] around, do not join. (*24 ch-sps*)

Rnd 3: [Ch 6, sc in **front lp** (*see Stitch Guide*) of next dc on rnd 1] around, sl st in next st. Fasten off, leaving a long tail.

FINISHING
With tail, sew Flower to side of Hat.

SCARF
HALF
MAKE 2.

Row 1: Beg at end of Scarf, ch 5, join with tr in first ch to form a ring, **ch 3** (see Pattern Notes), 6 dc in ring, turn. (7 dc)

Row 2: Ch 1, sc in first dc, [ch 3, sk next dc, sc in next dc] 3 times, turn. (3 ch-3 sps)

Row 3: (Sl st, ch 3, 2 dc) in first ch-3 sp, 3 dc in each of next 2 ch-3 sps, turn. (9 dc)

Row 4: Ch 1, sc in first dc, [ch 3, sk next dc, sc in next dc] 4 times, turn. (4 ch-3 sps)

Row 5: (Sl st, ch 3, dc) in first ch-3 sp, 2 dc in next ch-3 sp, dc in next sc, 2 dc in each of next 2 ch-3 sps, turn. (9 dc)

Next rows: Rep rows 4 and 5 until Scarf Half measures 9½ inches. At end of last row, fasten off.

FINISHING
Sew sts on last row of each Half tog for center back seam.

FINGERLESS GLOVES
BODY
MAKE 2.

Rnd 1 (RS): Ch 16, **join** (see Pattern Notes) in first ch to form a ring, **ch 3** (see Pattern Notes), dc in each rem ch around, join in 3rd ch of beg ch-3. (16 dc)

Rnd 2: Ch 3, **bpdc** (see Stitch Guide) around next dc, **fpdc** (see Stitch Guide) around each of next 2 dc, [bpdc around each of next 2 dc, fpdc around each of next 2 dc] around, join in 3rd ch of beg ch-3.

Rnd 3: Ch 1, sc in same ch as joining, ch 3, sk next 3 dc, sc in next dc, [ch 3, sk next 2 dc, sc in next dc] around to last 2 dc, ch 3, sk last 2 dc, join in first sc. (5 ch-3 sps)

Rnd 4: (Sl st, ch 3, 2 dc) in next ch-3 sp, 3 dc in each ch-3 sp around, join in 3rd ch of beg ch-3. (15 dc)

Rnd 5: **Ch 2** (see Pattern Notes), hdc in each of next 2 dc, ch 1, sk next dc (thumb opening made), hdc in each rem dc around, join in 2nd ch of beg ch-2. (14 dc, 1 ch-1 sp)

Rnd 6: Ch 1, sc in same ch as joining, [ch 3, sc in next hdc] twice, ch 3, sc in next ch-1 sp, [ch 3, sc in next hdc] around, ch 3, join in first sc. Fasten off. (15 ch-3 sps)

CHILD'S OUTFIT
HAT
BODY

Rnds 1–6: Rep rnds 1–6 on Doll's Hat. (68 sts)

Rnd 7: Ch 2, 3 dc in natural sp between next 2 dc, [hdc in each of next 2 hdc, 3 dc in natural sp between next 2 dc] around, hdc in last hdc, join in 2nd ch of beg ch-2. (85 sts)

SIZE SMALL/MEDIUM ONLY
Rnd 8: Ch 2, **hdc dec** (see Stitch Guide) in next 2 sts, hdc in each st around, join in 2nd ch of beg ch-2. (84 hdc)

SIZE MEDIUM/LARGE ONLY
Rnd [8]: Ch 2, [hdc in each next 15 sts, 2 hdc in next st] 5 times, hdc in each rem st around, join in 2nd ch of beg ch-2. ([90] hdc)

ALL SIZES
Rnd 9: Rep rnd 10 on Doll's Hat. (28 [30] ch-3 sps)

Rnd 10: Rep rnd 9 on Doll's Hat. (84 [90] sts)

Rnds 11–16 [11–18]: Rep last 2 rnds, 3 [4] times.

Rnd 17 [19]: Rep rnd 10 on Doll's Hat. Fasten off.

FLOWER
Rnds 1 & 2: Rep rnds 1 and 2 on Doll's Flower.

Rnd 3: [Ch 6, sc in **front lp** (see Stitch Guide) of next dc on rnd 1] around, do not join.

Rnd 4: [Ch 7, sc in **back lp** (see Stitch Guide) of next dc on rnd 1] around, sl st in next st. Fasten off, leaving a long tail.

FINISHING

With tail, sew Flower to side of Hat.

SCARF
HALF
MAKE 2.

Rows 1–5: Rep rows 1–5 on Doll's Scarf.

Rep rows 4 and 5 until Scarf Half measures 14 inches. Fasten off.

FINISHING

Sew sts on last row of each Half tog for center back seam.

FINGERLESS GLOVES
BODY
MAKE 2.

Rnd 1 (RS): Ch 28, **join** *(see Pattern Notes)* in first ch to form a ring, **ch 3** *(see Pattern Notes)*, dc in each rem ch around, join in 3rd ch of beg ch-3. *(28 dc)*

Rnds 2 & 3: Rep rnds 2 and 3 on Doll's Fingerless Gloves. *(9 ch-3 sps)*

Rnd 4: Rep rnd 4 on Doll's Fingerless Gloves. *(27 dc)*

Rnd 5: Ch 2 *(see Pattern Notes)*, hdc in each dc around, join in 2nd ch of beg ch-2.

Rnd 6: Ch 3, dc in each hdc around, join in 3rd ch of beg ch-3.

Rnd 7: Ch 2, hdc in each of next 2 dc, ch 2, sk next 2 dc *(thumb opening made)*, hdc in each rem dc around, join in 2nd ch of beg ch-2. *(25 hdc, 1 ch-2 sp)*

Rnd 8: Ch 3, dc in each of next 2 hdc, 2 dc in next ch-2 sp, dc in each rem hdc around, join in 3rd ch of beg ch-3. *(27 dc)*

Rnd 9: Ch 1, sc in same ch as joining, [ch 3, sc in next dc] around, ch 3, join in first sc. Fasten off. *(27 ch-3 sps)* ∎

Cutie Pie Curlicue
Hat, Scarf & Fingerless Gloves
DESIGNS BY **SUE CHILDRESS**

SKILL LEVEL

INTERMEDIATE

FINISHED SIZES

Doll: Fits 18-inch fashion doll
Child: Instructions given fit child's size small/medium; changes for child's size medium/large are in [ ].

FINISHED GARMENT MEASUREMENTS

Child's Hat: Approximately 18 [20] inches in circumference
Child's Scarf: 24 inches long
Child's Fingerless Gloves: 6 [6¾] inches in circumference x 3½ [3¾] inches long
Doll's Scarf: 15 inches long

MATERIALS

- Sport weight cotton yarn:
  250 yds variegated
- Size F/5/3.75mm crochet hook
  or size needed to obtain gauge
- Tapestry needle

2 FINE

GAUGE

9 sts = 2 inches

Take time to check gauge.

PATTERN NOTES

Weave in ends as work progresses.

Join with slip stitch as indicated unless
  otherwise stated.

Chain-3 at beginning of round counts as first
  double crochet, front post double crochet
  or back post double crochet unless
  otherwise stated.

Chain-2 at beginning of round counts as first
  half double crochet unless otherwise stated.

DOLL'S OUTFIT
HAT
BODY

Rnd 1 (RS): Ch 6, **join** *(see Pattern Notes)* in 6th ch from hook to form a ring, **ch 3** *(see Pattern Notes)*, 19 dc in ring, join in 3rd ch of beg ch-3. *(20 dc)*

Rnd 2: Ch 3, **fpdc** *(see Stitch Guide)* around next dc, **bpdc** *(see Stitch Guide)* around each of next 2 dc, [fpdc around each of next 2 dc, bpdc around each of next 2 dc] around, join in 3rd ch of beg ch-3. *(10 fpdc, 10 bpdc)*

Rnd 3: Ch 3, 2 dc in next dc, [dc in next dc, 2 dc in next dc] around, join in 3rd ch of beg ch-3. *(30 dc)*

Rnd 4: Ch 3, 2 fpdc around each of next 2 dc, [dc in next dc, 2 fpdc around each of next 2 dc] around, join in 3rd ch of beg ch-3. *(40 fpdc, 10 dc)*

Rnd 5: Ch 3, dc in each of next 3 dc, 2 dc in next dc, [dc in each of next 4 dc, 2 dc in next dc] around, join in 3rd ch of beg ch-3. *(60 dc)*

Rnds 6–8: Ch 2 *(see Pattern Notes)*, hdc in each st around, join in 2nd ch of beg ch-2. *(60 hdc)*

Rnd 9: Ch 3, bpdc around next hdc, fpdc around each of next 2 hdc, [bpdc around each of next 2 hdc, fpdc around each of next 2 hdc] around, join in 3rd ch of beg ch-3. *(30 fpdc, 30 bpdc)*

Rnds 10 & 11: Ch 3, bpdc around next bpdc, fpdc around each of next 2 fpdc, [bpdc around each of next 2 bpdc, fpdc around each of next 2 fpdc] around, join in 3rd ch of beg ch-3. At end of rnd 11, fasten off.

CURLICUE
MAKE 4.
Leaving 2-inch tail, ch 20, working in only 1 lp of each ch, 3 sc in 2nd ch from hook, 3 sc in each rem ch across. Leaving 2-inch tail, fasten off.

FINISHING
Tie tails of Curlicue to top center of Hat.

SCARF
Ch 120, working in only 1 lp of each ch, (sc, ch 1) 3 times in 2nd ch from hook, (sc, ch 1) 3 times in each rem ch across. Fasten off.

FINGERLESS GLOVES
RIGHT GLOVE
Rnd 1 (RS): Ch 20, **join** *(see Pattern Notes)* in first ch to form a ring, **ch 3** *(see Pattern Notes)*, dc in each ch around, join in 3rd ch of beg ch-3. *(20 dc)*

Rnd 2: Ch 3, **fpdc** *(see Stitch Guide)* around next dc, [**bpdc** *(see Stitch Guide)* around next dc, fpdc around next dc] around, join in 3rd ch of beg ch-3. *(10 fpdc, 10 bpdc)*

Rnds 3–6: Ch 3, fpdc around next fpdc, [bpdc around next bpdc, fpdc around next fpdc] around, join in 3rd ch of beg ch-3.

Rnd 7: Ch 3, dc in next 2 dc, ch 1, sk next dc, *(thumb opening made)*, dc in each rem dc around, join in 3rd ch of beg ch-3. *(19 dc, 1 ch-1 sp)*

Rnd 8: Ch 1, sc in same ch as joining, sc in each of next 2 dc, sc in next ch-1 sp, sc in each rem dc around, join in first sc. *(20 sc)*

Rnd 9: Ch 1, sc in same st as joining, *ch 9, working in only 1 lp of each ch, 3 sc in 2nd ch from hook, 3 sc in each rem ch *(Curlicue made)*, sc in same st as joining, rep from * once, sc in each rem sc around, join in first sc. Fasten off. *(21 sc, 2 Curlicues)*

LEFT GLOVE
Rnds 1–8: Rep rnds 1–8 on Right Glove.

Rnd 9: Ch 1, sc in same st as joining, sc in each of next 4 sc, *ch 9, working in only 1 lp of each ch, 3 sc in 2nd ch from hook, 3 sc in each rem ch *(Curlicue made)*, sc in same st as last sc made before ch-9, rep from * once, sc in each rem sc around, join in first sc. Fasten off. *(21 sc, 2 Curlicues)*

CHILD'S OUTFIT
HAT
BODY
Rnds 1–5: Rep rnds 1–5 of Doll's Hat.

Rnd 6: Ch 3, dc in each of next 3 dc, 2 fpdc around each of next 2 dc, [dc in each of next 4 dc, 2 fpdc around each of next 2 dc] around, join in 3rd ch of beg ch-3. *(40 fpdc, 40 dc)*

Rnd 7: Ch 3, dc in each st around, join in 3rd ch of beg ch-3. *(80 dc)*

SIZE SMALL/MEDIUM ONLY
Rnd 8: Ch 3, dc in each of next 6 dc, fpdc around next dc, [dc in each of next 7 dc, fpdc around next dc] around, join in 3rd ch of beg ch-3. *(10 fpdc, 70 dc)*

Rnd 9: Ch 3, fpdc around each of next 2 sts, bpdc around each of next 2 sts, [fpdc around each of next 3 sts, bpdc around each of next 2 sts] around, join in 3rd ch of beg ch-3. *(48 fpdc, 32 bpdc)*

Rnds 10–12: Ch 3, fpdc around each of next 2 fpdc, bpdc around each of next 2 bpdc, [fpdc around each of next 3 fpdc, bpdc around each of next 2 bpdc] around, join in 3rd ch of beg ch-3.

Rnds 13–15: Ch 2 *(see Pattern Notes)*, hdc in each st around, join in 2nd ch of beg ch-2. *(80 hdc)*

Rnd 16: Ch 3, fpdc around next hdc, bpdc around each of next 2 hdc, [fpdc around each of next 2 hdc, bpdc around each of next 2 hdc] around, join in 3rd ch of beg ch-3. *(40 fpdc, 40 bpdc)*

Rnds 17 & 18: Ch 3, fpdc around next fpdc, bpdc around each of next 2 bpdc, [fpdc around each of next 2 fpdc, bpdc around each of next 2 bpdc] around, join in 3rd ch of beg ch-3. At end of rnd 18, fasten off.

SIZE MEDIUM/LARGE ONLY
Rnd [8]: Ch 3, dc in each of next 6 dc, 2 fpdc around next dc, [dc in next 7 dc, 2 fpdc around next dc] around, join in 3rd ch of beg ch-3. *([20] fpdc, [70] dc)*

Rnd [9]: Ch 3, fpdc around each of next 2 sts, bpdc around each of next 3 sts, [fpdc around each of next 3 sts, bpdc around each of next 3 sts] around, join in 3rd ch of beg ch-3. *([45] fpdc, [45] bpdc)*

Rnds [10–14]: Ch 3, fpdc around each of next 2 fpdc, bpdc around each of next 3 bpdc, [fpdc around each of next 3 fpdc, bpdc around each of next 3 bpdc] around, join in 3rd ch of beg ch-3.

Rnds [15–17]: **Ch 2** *(see Pattern Notes)*, hdc in each st around, join in 2nd ch of beg ch-2. *([90] hdc)*

Rnd [18]: Ch 3, fpdc around next hdc, [bpdc around each of next 2 hdc, fpdc around each of next 2 hdc] around, join in 3rd ch of beg ch-3. *([46] fpdc, [44] bpdc)*

Rnds [19 & 20]: Ch 3, fpdc around next fpdc, [bpdc around each of next 2 bpdc, fpdc around each of next 2 fpdc] around, join in 3rd ch of beg ch-3. At end of rnd 20, fasten off.

SHORT CURLICUE
MAKE 4.
Work same as Doll's Hat Curlicue.

LONG CURLICUE
MAKE 4.
Leaving 2-inch tail, ch 24, working in only 1 lp of each ch, 3 sc in 2nd ch from hook, 3 sc in each rem ch across. Leaving 2-inch tail, fasten off.

FINISHING
Tie tails of all 8 Curlicues to top center of Hat.

SCARF
Ch 150, working in only 1 lp of each ch, (dc, ch 1) 5 times in 4th ch from hook, (dc, ch 1) 5 times in each rem ch across. Fasten off.

FINGERLESS GLOVES
MAKE 2.
Rnd 1 (RS): Ch 36 [40], **join** *(see Pattern Notes)* in first ch to form a ring, **ch 3** *(see Pattern Notes)*, dc in each ch around, join in 3rd ch of beg ch-3. *(36 [40] dc)*

Rnd 2: Ch 3, **bpdc** (*see Stitch Guide)* around next dc, **fpdc** (*see Stitch Guide)* around each of next 2 dc, [bpdc around each of next 2 dc, fpdc around each of next 2 dc] around, join in 3rd ch of beg ch-3. *(18 [20] fpdc, 18 [20] bpdc)*

Rnds 3–7 [3–8]: Ch 3, bpdc around next bpdc, fpdc around each of next 2 fpdc, [bpdc around each of next 2 bpdc, fpdc around each of next 2 fpdc] around, join in 3rd ch of beg ch-3.

Rnd 8 [9]: Ch 3, dc in each of next 3 sts, ch 2, sk next 2 sts (*thumb opening made)*, dc in each rem st around, join in 3rd ch of beg ch-3. *(34 [38] dc, ch-2 sp)*

Rnd 9 [10]: Ch 3, dc in each of next 3 dc, 2 dc in next ch-2 sp, dc in each rem dc around, join in 3rd ch of beg ch-3. *(36 [40] dc)*

Rnds 10 & 11 [11 & 12]: Rep rnds 2 and 3. At end of last rnd, fasten off. ∎

Pink Parfait
Hat, Scarf & Fingerless Gloves
DESIGNS BY **FRANCES HUGHES**

SKILL LEVEL

INTERMEDIATE

FINISHED SIZES
Doll: Fits 18-inch fashion doll
Child: Instructions given fit child's size small/medium; changes for child's size medium/large are in [ ].

FINISHED GARMENT MEASUREMENTS
Child's Hat: Approximately 17 [18½] inches in circumference
Child's Scarf: 18½ x 1¾ inches, including Curlicues
Child's Fingerless Gloves: 5½ [6½] inches in circumference x 3½ inches long
Doll's Scarf: 15½ x 1¼ inch, including Curlicues

MATERIALS
- Sock weight yarn:
  460 yds pink variegated

1 SUPER FINE

- Sizes C/2/2.75mm and G/6/4mm crochet hooks or sizes needed to obtain gauge
- Tapestry needle

GAUGE
With size C hook and 1 strand of yarn: 11 sts = 2 inches

With size G hook and 2 strands of yarn held tog: 8 sts = 2 inches

Take time to check gauge.

PATTERN NOTES
Weave in ends as work progresses.

Join with slip stitch as indicated unless otherwise stated.

Chain-3 at beginning of row or round counts as first double crochet unless otherwise stated.

Chain-2 at beginning of round counts as first half double crochet unless otherwise stated.

Use size C hook and 1 strand of yarn for doll's projects. Use size G hook and 2 strands of yarn for child's projects.

DOLL'S OUTFIT
HAT
BODY

Rnd 1 (RS): With size C hook and 1 strand of yarn throughout, ch 4, **join** *(see Pattern Notes)* in first ch to form a ring, **ch 3** *(see Pattern Notes)*, 11 dc in ring, join in 3rd ch of beg ch-3. *(12 dc)*

Rnd 2: Ch 3, dc in same dc as joining, 2 dc in each dc around, join in 3rd ch of beg ch-3. *(24 dc)*

Rnd 3: Ch 3, dc in same dc as joining, dc in next dc, [2 dc in next dc, dc in next dc] around, join in 3rd ch of beg ch-3. *(36 dc)*

Rnd 4: Ch 3, dc in next dc, 2 dc in next dc, [dc in each of next 2 dc, 2 dc in next dc] around, join in 3rd ch of beg ch-3. *(48 dc)*

Rnd 5: Ch 3, dc in same dc as joining, dc in each of next 3 dc, [2 dc in next dc, dc in each of next 3 dc] around, join in 3rd ch of beg ch-3. *(60 dc)*

Rnds 6–13: Ch 3, dc in each dc around, join in 3rd ch of beg ch-3.

FIRST EARFLAP

Row 1: Now working in rows, ch 3, dc in each of next 18 dc, turn. *(19 dc)*

Row 2: Ch 3, **dc dec** *(see Stitch Guide)* in next 2 sts, dc in each of next 9 dc, turn. Leave rem sts unworked. *(11 dc)*

Row 3: Ch 3, dc dec in next 2 sts, dc in each dc across, turn. Leave beg ch-3 unworked. *(9 dc)*

Rows 4–6: Rep row 3. *(3 dc)*

Row 7: Ch 2 *(does not count as a st)*, dc dec in next 2 sts. *(1 dc)*

CURLICUE
Ch 25, working in only 1 lp of each ch, 3 sc in 2nd ch from hook, 3 sc in each rem ch across, join in st on row 7. Fasten off.

2ND EARFLAP
Row 1: With WS facing, join yarn in 3rd ch of beg ch-3 on row 1 of First Earflap, working in sts on rnd 13, dc in each of next 19 dc, turn. *(19 dc)*

Rows 2–7: Rep rows 2–7 of First Earflap.

CURLICUE
Rep Curlicue of First Earflap.

TOP CURLICUE
Leaving long tail, with size C hook, ch 35, working in only 1 lp of each ch, 3 sc in 2nd ch from hook, 3 sc in each rem ch across. Fasten off, leaving a long tail.

FINISHING
Sew Top Curlicue to top center of Hat.

SCARF
FIRST CURLICUE
With size C hook and 1 strand of yarn, ch 20, working in only 1 lp of each ch, 3 sc in 2nd ch from hook, 3 sc in each rem ch across, turn.

BODY
Row 1: Ch 1, 2 sc in first sc of Curlicue, sc in next sc, turn. Leave rem sts on Curlicue unworked. *(3 sc)*

Row 2: Ch 1, 2 sc in first sc, sc in next sc, 2 sc in last sc, turn. *(5 sc)*

Row 3: Ch 1, sc in each sc across, turn.

Row 4: Ch 1, 2 sc in first sc, sc in each of next 3 sc, 2 sc in last sc, turn. *(7 sc)*

Row 5: **Ch 3** *(see Pattern Notes)*, dc in each st across, turn. *(7 dc)*

Rep row 5 until Body measures approximately 12½ inches long, excluding Curlicue.

Next 2 rows: Ch 1, **sc dec** *(see Stitch Guide)* in next 2 sts, sc in each st across to last 2 sts, sc dec in last 2 sts, turn. *(3 sts)*

Last row: Ch 1, sc dec in next 3 sts. *(1 st)*

2ND CURLICUE
Ch 20, working in only 1 lp of each ch, 3 sc in 2nd ch from hook, 3 sc in each rem ch across, join in st on last row. Fasten off.

FINGERLESS GLOVES
MAKE 2.
BODY
Rnd 1 (RS): With size C hook and 1 strand of yarn, ch 20, **join** *(see Pattern Notes)* in first ch to form a ring, **ch 2** *(see Pattern Notes)*, hdc in each rem ch around, join in 2nd ch of beg ch-2. *(20 hdc)*

Rnds 2 & 3: Ch 2, hdc in each hdc around, join in 2nd ch of beg ch-2.

Rnd 4: Ch 2, hdc in each of next 4 hdc, ch 2, sk next 2 hdc *(thumb opening made)*, hdc in each rem hdc around, join in 2nd ch of beg ch-2. *(18 hdc, 1 ch-2 sp)*

Rnd 5: Ch 2, hdc in each of next 4 hdc, 2 hdc in ch-2 sp, hdc in each rem hdc around, join in 2nd ch of beg ch-2. *(20 hdc)*

Rnds 6–8: Rep rnd 2.

CURLICUE
Ch 8, working in only 1 lp of each ch, 3 sc in 2nd ch from hook, 3 sc in each rem ch across, join in st at base of Curlicue. Fasten off.

CHILD'S OUTFIT
HAT
BODY
Rnds 1–5 (RS): With size G hook and 2 strands of yarn throughout, rep rnds 1–5 of Doll's Hat. *(60 dc)*

SIZE SMALL/MEDIUM ONLY
Rnd 6: Ch 3, dc in each of next 8 dc, 2 dc in next dc, [dc in each of next 9 dc, 2 dc in next dc] around, join in 3rd ch of beg ch-3. *(66 dc)*

Rnds 7–13: Ch 3, dc in each dc around, join in 3rd ch of beg ch-3.

Work First Earflap, 2nd Earflap and Curlicues same as Doll's Hat.

TOP CURLICUE
Work Top Curlicue same as Doll's Hat.

FINISHING
Sew Top Curlicue to top center of Hat.

SIZE MEDIUM/LARGE ONLY
Rnd [6]: Ch 3, dc in same dc as joining, dc in each of next 4 dc, [2 dc in next dc, dc in each of next 4 dc] around, join in 3rd ch of beg ch-3. ([72] dc)

Rnds [7–14]: Ch 3, dc in each dc around, join in 3rd ch of beg ch-3.

FIRST EARFLAP
Row [1]: Now working in rows, ch 3, dc in each of next 19 dc, turn. ([20] dc)

Rows [2–7]: Rep rows 2–7 on First Earflap of Doll's Hat.

Work Curlicue same as Doll's Hat.

2ND EARFLAP
Row [1]: With WS facing, join yarn in 3rd ch of beg ch-3 on row 1 of First Earflap, working in sts on rnd 13, dc in each of next 20 dc, turn. ([20] dc)

Rows [2–7]: Rep rows 2–7 on First Earflap of Doll's Hat.

TOP CURLICUE
Work Top Curlicue same as Doll's Hat.

FINISHING
Sew Top Curlicue to top center of Hat.

SCARF
FIRST CURLICUE
With size G hook and 2 strands of yarn held tog, ch 20, working in only 1 lp of each ch, 3 sc in 2nd ch from hook, 3 sc in each rem ch across, turn.

BODY
Row 1: Ch 1, 2 sc in first sc of Curlicue, sc in next sc, turn. Leave rem sts on Curlicue unworked. (3 sc)

Row 2: Ch 1, 2 sc in first sc, sc in next sc, 2 sc in last sc, turn. (5 sc)

Row 3: Ch 1, sc in each sc across, turn.

Row 4: Ch 1, 2 sc in first sc, sc in each of next 3 sc, 2 sc in last sc, turn. (7 sc)

Row 5: **Ch 3** (see Pattern Notes), dc in each st across, turn. (7 dc)

Rep row 5 until piece measures approximately 14 inches long, excluding Curlicue.

Next 2 rows: Ch 1, **sc dec** (see Stitch Guide) in next 2 sts, sc in each st across to last 2 sts, sc dec in last 2 sts, turn. (3 sts)

Last row: Ch 1, sc dec in next 3 sts. (1 st)

2ND CURLICUE
Ch 20, working in only 1 lp of each ch, 3 sc in 2nd ch from hook, 3 sc in each rem ch across, join in st on last row. Fasten off.

FINGERLESS GLOVES
MAKE 2.
Rnd 1 (RS): With size G hook and 2 strands of yarn, ch 22 [26], **join** (see Pattern Notes) in first ch to form a ring, **ch 3** (see Pattern Notes), dc in each rem ch around, join in 3rd ch of beg ch-3. (22 [26] dc)

Rnds 2 & 3: Ch 3, dc in each dc around, join in 3rd ch of beg ch-3.

Rnd 4: Ch 3, dc in next 4 dc, ch 2, sk next 2 dc (thumb opening made), dc in each rem dc around, join in 3rd ch of beg ch-3. (20 [24] dc, 1 ch-2 sp)

Rnd 5: Ch 3, dc in each of next 4 dc, 2 dc in ch-2 sp, dc in each rem dc around, join in 3rd ch of beg ch-3. (22 [26] dc)

Rnds 6–8: Rep rnd 2.

CURLICUE
Rep Curlicue of Doll's Fingerless Gloves. ■

Slippers

DESIGNS BY **SUE CHILDRESS**

SKILL LEVEL
INTERMEDIATE

FINISHED SIZES
Doll: Fits 18-inch fashion doll
Child: Instructions given fit 6-inch foot *(small)*; changes for 7-inch foot *(medium)* and 8-inch foot *(large)* are in [ ].

FINISHED GARMENT MEASUREMENTS
Doll's sole: 2½ inches long
Child's sole: 6 [7, 8] inches long

MATERIALS
- Patons Canadiana medium (worsted) weight yarn (solid: 3½ oz/ 205 yds/100g per ball; ombre: 3½ oz/192 yds/100g per ball):
    1 ball #10420 cherished pink *(MC)*
    1 ball #11420 pretty baby *(CC)*
- Size F/5/3.75mm crochet hook or size needed to obtain gauge
- Buttons:
    ⅝ inch: 2
    ⅜ inch: 2

GAUGE
4 sts = 1 inch

PATTERN NOTE
Join with slip stitch as indicated unless otherwise stated.

DOLL'S SLIPPER
SOLE & BODY
MAKE 2.
Rnd 1: With MC, ch 8, hdc in 3rd ch from hook, hdc each of next 3 chs, 2 hdc in next ch, 5 dc in last ch, working on opposite side of ch, 2 hdc in next ch, hdc in each of next 4 chs, **do not join or turn.**

Rnd 2: 2 sc in 2nd ch of beg 2 sk chs, sc in each of next 4 hdc, hdc in each of next 2 hdc, [2 dc in next dc, dc in next dc] 3 times, hdc in next dc, sc in each of next 5 sts, **join** *(see Pattern Note)* in first sc.

Rnd 3: Ch 1, sc in each st around, join in first sc. *(24 sc)*

Rnd 4: Ch 2, **bpdc** *(see Stitch Guide)* around each sc around, join in 2nd ch of beg ch-2.

Rnd 5: Ch 2, hdc in each of next 7 hdc, [**dc dec** *(see Stitch Guide)* in next 2 sts] 5 times, hdc in each rem st around, join in beg ch-2.

RIGHT SLIPPER STRAP
Rnd 6: Ch 1, sc in each of next 6 hdc, ch 9, sc in 5th ch from hook *(button lp)*, sc in each rem ch across, sc in same hdc as 6th sc on rnd 5 of Slipper, working in rnd 5 of Body, sc in each rem hdc around, join in beg ch-1. Fasten off.

LEFT SLIPPER STRAP
Rnd 6: Ch 1, sc in each of next 15 hdc, ch 9, sc in 5th ch from hook *(button lp)*, sc in each ch rem ch across, sc in same hdc as 15th sc on rnd 5 of Slipper, working in rnd 5 of Body, sc in each rem hdc around, join in beg ch-1. Fasten off.

FINISHING
Use button lp to determine button position and sew ⅜-inch button to Slipper side.

FLOWER
MAKE 2.
Rnd 1: With CC, ch 4, join in 4th ch from hook to form a ring, [ch 4, sc in ring] 9 times, join in top of beg ch-4. Fasten off.

CHILD'S SLIPPER
SOLE & BODY
MAKE 2.
Rnd 1: With MC, ch 16 [20, 24], 2 hdc in 3rd ch from hook, sc in each ch around to last 2 chs, 2 hdc in next ch, 5 dc in last ch, working in rem lps on opposite side of ch, 2 hdc in next ch, sc in each ch around to last ch, 2 hdc in last ch, **do not join or turn.** (35 [43, 51] sts)

Rnd 2: 2 hdc in 2nd ch of beg 2 sk chs, 2 hdc in each of next 2 hdc, 2 sc in next sc, sc in each st around to 5-dc group, 2 dc in each of next 5 dc, sc in each rem st around, **join** (see Pattern Note) in first hdc. (44 [52, 60] sts)

Rnd 3: Ch 2, hdc in same hdc as beg ch-2, 2 hdc in each of next 3 sts, hdc in each rem st around to 10-dc group, [2 hdc in next dc, hdc in next dc] 5 times, hdc in each st around to last 4 sts, 2 hdc in each of next 3 sts, hdc in last st, join in top of beg ch-2. (56 [64, 72] hdc)

SIDE
Rnd 4: Ch 3, **bpdc** (see Stitch Guide) around each hdc around, join in beg ch-3. (56 [64, 72] sts)

Rnd 5: Ch 3, bpdc around next bpdc, **fpdc** (see Stitch Guide) around each of next 2 bpdc, [bpdc around each of next 2 bpdc, fpdc around each of next 2 bpdc] around, join in top of beg ch-3.

Rnd 6: Ch 3, bpdc around next st, fpdc around each of next 2 st, *[bpdc around each of next 2 st, fpdc around each of next 2 st] 4 [5, 6] times*, [**tr dec** (see Stitch Guide) in next 2 sts] 9 times, [fpdc around each of next 2 st, bpdc around each of next 2 st] 4 [5, 6] times, fpdc around each of next 2 st, join in top of beg ch-3.

Rnd 7: Ch 2, hdc in each of next 17 [21, 26] sts [**dc dec** (see Stitch Guide) in next 2 sts] 7 times, hdc in each rem st around, join in top of beg ch-2. (40 [48, 55] sts)

SIZES MEDIUM & LARGE ONLY
Rnd [8, 8]: Ch 2, hdc in each st around to last 2 hdc before dc dec, [dc dec in next 2 sts] 6 times, hdc in each rem st around, join in top of beg ch-2. ([42, 50] sts)

RIGHT SLIPPER STRAP
Rnd 8 [9, 9]: Ch 1, sc in each of next 12 [14, 18] hdc, ch 14, sc in 5th ch from hook (button lp), sc in each rem ch across, sc in next hdc of rnd 8 of Slipper, working in rnd 7 of Body, sc in each rem hdc around, join in beg ch-1. Fasten off.

LEFT SLIPPER STRAP
Rnd 8 [9, 9]: Join MC in 29th st of row 7, ch 1, sc in each of next 30 [32, 38] hdc, ch 14, sc in 5th ch from hook (button lp), sc in each ch rem ch across, sc in next hdc of rnd 8 of Slipper, sc in each rem hdc around, join in beg ch-1. Fasten off.

FINISHING
Use button lp to determine button position and sew 3/8-inch button to Slipper side.

FLOWER
MAKE 2.
Rnd 1: With CC, ch 4, join in 4th ch from hook to form a ring, ch 3, 14 dc in ring, join in top of beg ch-3.

Rnd 2: [Ch 5, **fpsc** (see Stitch Guide) around next dc] around, ch 5, join at base of beg ch-5. Fasten off. ∎

Messenger Bag

DESIGNS BY **FRANCES HUGHES**

SKILL LEVEL

EASY

FINISHED SIZES

Doll's Bag: 4¾ x 5 inches, with Flap down and excluding Strap

Child's Bag: 8¼ x 9½ inches, with Flap down and excluding Strap

MATERIALS

- Plymouth Yarn Fantasy Naturale medium (worsted) weight yarn (3½ oz/140 yds/100g per hank): 2 hanks #1404 bright gold
- Size G/6/4mm crochet hook or size needed to obtain gauge
- ⅜-inch snap
- 1-inch number buttons

GAUGE

4 hdc = 1 inch; 4 hdc rows = 2 inches

DOLL'S BAG
BODY & FLAP

Row 1: Ch 19, hdc in 3rd ch from hook and in each rem ch across, turn. (*17 hdc*)

Row 2 (RS): Working in **back lps** (*see Stitch Guide*), ch 2, hdc in first hdc and in each rem hdc across, turn. (*17 hdc*)

Rows 3–16: Rep row 2.

Row 17: Ch 2, hdc in first hdc and in each of next 12 hdc, sc in each of last 4 hdc, turn.

Row 18: Ch 1, sc in each of next 4 sts, hdc in each of next 3 hdc, dc in each of next 10 hdc, **do not fasten off or turn**.

BORDER

Ch 2, working in ends of rows, 2 hdc in end of each of next 4 rows, fold row 1 up and align with row 14, working through both thicknesses, 2 hdc in end of each row across to fold, 3 hdc in end of last row, hdc in each rem lp across bottom, working through both thicknesses, work 3 hdc in opposite end of last row, 2 hdc in end of each row across to Flap, 2 hdc in end of each rem row, working in row 18, sc in each st across, join with sl st in top of beg ch-2.

FINISHING

Sew ½ of snap to asymmetrical corner of Flap. Align and sew rem ½ to upper right side of Bag front. Sew buttons in place as shown in photo or as desired.

STRAP

Ch 65, hdc in 3rd ch from hook (*beg 2 sk chs count as first hdc*) and each rem ch across. Fasten off.

Sew Strap to Bag at fold of Flap.

CHILD'S BAG
BODY & FLAP

Row 1: Ch 35, hdc in 3rd ch from hook and in each rem ch across, turn. (*33 hdc*)

Row 2 (RS): Working in **back lps** (*see Stitch Guide*), ch 2, hdc in first hdc and in each rem hdc across, turn. (*33 hdc*)

Rows 3–35: Rep row 2.

Row 36: Ch 1, sc in each of next 11 hdc, hdc in each of next 22 hdc, turn.

Row 37: Ch 2, hdc in each of next 22 hdc, sc in each of next 11 sc, turn.

Row 38: Ch 1, sc in each of next 11 sc, hdc in each of next 3 hdc, dc in each of next 19 hdc, **do not fasten off or turn.**

BORDER
Ch 2, working in ends of rows, 2 hdc in end of each of next 7 rows, fold row 1 up and align with row 30, working through both thicknesses, 2 hdc in end of each row across to fold, 3 hdc in end of last row, hdc in each rem lp across bottom, working through both thicknesses, work 3 hdc in opposite end of last row, 2 hdc in end of each row across to flap, 2 hdc in end of each rem row, working in row 38, sc in each st across, join with sl st in top of beg ch-2.

FINISHING
Sew ½ of snap to asymmetrical corner of Flap. Align and sew rem ½ to upper right side of Bag front. Sew buttons in place as shown in photo or as desired.

STRAP
Row 1: Ch 94, hdc in 3rd ch from hook and in each ch across, turn.

Row 2: Ch 2, hdc in each hdc across. Fasten off.

Sew Strap to Bag at fold of Flap. ∎

Crocheted Dog
Dog Bed, Blanket & Toy
DESIGNS BY **FRANCES HUGHES**

SKILL LEVEL

EASY

FINISHED SIZES
Dog: Approximately 4 inches long
Dog Bed: 9½ inches in diameter
Blanket: 10½ x 11 inches
Dog Toy: Approximately 2¼ inches long, including bells

MATERIALS
- Fine (sport) weight yarn:
  50 yds each fuchsia, pale green, coral, yellow and green/yellow/orange variegated
- Light (DK) weight yarn:
  178 yds each black and white
- Medium (worsted) weight yarn:
  185 yds each tan and orange-red
- Embroidery floss:
  18 inches each brown and red
- Sizes E/4/3.5mm, F/5/3.75mm, H/8/5mm and I/9/5.5mm crochet hooks or sizes needed to obtain gauge
- Tapestry needle
- 2 small jingle bells *(optional)*
- Small bead or charm *(optional)*
- ¼-inch-wide ribbon: 8-inches
- Polyester fiberfill
- Stitch marker

GAUGE
Size E hook and fine weight yarn: 6 sts = 1 inch

Size F hook and lightweight yarn: 5 sc = 1 inch

Size H hook and medium weight yarn: 4 sts = 1 inch

Size I hook and 2 strands medium weight yarn held tog: Rnds 1 and 2 = 1¾ inches

PATTERN NOTES
Do not join rounds unless otherwise stated. Place stitch marker at beginning of round. Move marker as work progresses.

When told to join, join with slip stitch as indicated unless otherwise stated.

DOG
BODY
Rnd 1: With white and F hook, ch 4, **join** *(see Pattern Notes)* in 4th ch from hook to form a ring, ch 1, 10 sc in ring, **do not join** *(see Pattern Notes)*, **mark beg of rnd** *(see Pattern Notes)*.

Rnd 2: 2 sc in each sc around. *(20 sc)*

Rnd 3: 2 sc in first sc, sc in next sc, [2 sc in next sc, sc in next sc] around. *(30 sc)*

Rnds 4–17: Sc in each sc around.

Rnd 18 (dec): [**Sc dec** *(see Stitch Guide)* in next 2 sts, sc in next sc] around. *(20 sc)*

Stuff lightly with fiberfill.

Rnds 19 & 20: [Sc dec in next 2 sts] around. Fasten off. *(5 sc)*

MUZZLE & HEAD
Rnd 1: With white and size F hook, ch 2, 7 sc in 2nd ch from hook, do not join, mark beg of rnd.

Rnd 2: 2 sc in each st around. *(14 sc)*

Rnds 3 & 4: Sc in each st around, **change color** *(see Stitch Guide)* to black at end of last rnd. *(14 sc)*

Rnd 5: 2 sc in each st around.

Rnds 6–12: Sc in each st around.

Rnds 13 & 14: [Sc dec in next 2 sts] around. At end of last rnd, fasten off. *(7 sc at end of last rnd)*

EARS
MAKE 2.
Row 1: With white and size F hook, ch 4, sc in 2nd ch from hook and in each of next 2 chs, turn. *(3 sc)*

Rows 2 & 3: Ch 1, 2 sc in first sc, sc in each of next 2 sc, turn. *(5 sc)*

Row 4: Ch 1, sc in each sc across, turn.

Row 5: Ch 1, sc dec in first 2 sts, sc in next sc, sc dec in last 2 sts, turn. *(3 sc)*

Row 6: Sc dec in 3 sts. Fasten off.

FRONT LEGS
MAKE 2.
Rnd 1: With white and size F hook, ch 2, 5 sc in 2nd ch from hook, do not join, mark beg of rnd.

Rnd 2: 2 sc in each sc around. *(10 sc)*

Rnds 3 & 4: Sc in each sc around.

Rnd 5: Join black in first st, [sc dec in next 2 sts, sc in next sc] 3 times, sc in last sc. *(7 sc)*

Rnds 6–12: Sc in each sc around. At end of last rnd, stuff lightly, set aside.

BACK LEGS
MAKE 2.
Rnds 1–10: Rep rnds 1–10 of Front Legs. At end of last rnd, stuff lightly, set aside.

HAUNCHES
MAKE 2.
Rnd 1: With white and F hook, ch 2, join in 2nd ch from hook to form a ring, 5 sc in ring.

Rnd 2: 2 sc in each sc around.

Rnd 3: [2 sc in next sc, sc in next sc] around. Fasten off. *(15 sc)*

TAIL
With size F hook and black, ch 8, hdc in 2nd ch from hook and each rem ch across. Fasten off. *(7 hdc)*

FINISHING
Safety note: If intended recipient is 4 years of age or younger, do not attach bead or charm to ribbon.

Sew Haunches to Back Legs. Sew assembled Back Legs, Tail and Front Legs to Body. Sew Ears to Head. Sew Head to Body.

With black and using **satin stitch** *(see illustration)*, stitch nose as shown in photo.

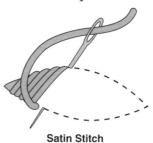

Satin Stitch

With 3 strands red embroidery floss held tog and using **straight stitch** *(see illustration)*, stitch mouth below nose as shown in photo.

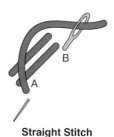

Straight Stitch

With 3 strands brown embroidery floss held tog and using satin stitch, stitch eyes as shown in photo.

With 1 ply light-weight white yarn, using satin stitch, add eye accent as shown in photo.

Optional *(see Safety Note)*: Make a dog tag with ribbon and small bead or charm. Tie ribbon around neck.

DOG BED
Rnd 1: With size I hook and 2 strands tan held tog, ch 4, join in 4th ch from hook to form ring, ch 1, 10 sc in ring, **do not join** *(see Pattern Notes)*, **mark beg of rnd** *(see Pattern Notes)*.

Rnd 2: 2 sc in each sc around. *(20 sc)*

Rnd 3: [2 sc in next sc, sc in next sc] around. *(30 sc)*

Rnd 4: [2 sc in next sc, sc in each of next 2 sc] around. *(40 sc)*

Rnd 5: [2 sc in next sc, sc in each of next 3 sc] around. *(50 sc)*

Rnd 6: [2 sc in next sc, sc in each of next 4 sc] around. *(60 sc)*

Rnd 7: [2 sc in next sc, sc in each of next 5 sc] around. *(70 sc)*

Rnd 8: [2 sc in next sc, sc in each of next 6 sc] around. *(80 sc)*

Rnd 9: [2 sc in next sc, sc in each of next 7 sc] around. *(90 sc)*

Rnd 10: [2 sc in next sc, sc in each of next 8 sc] around. *(100 sc)*

Rnd 11: Working in **back lps** *(see Stitch Guide)*, sc in each sc around. Fasten off tan.

Rnd 12: With 2 strands orange-red held tog, working in rem lps of rnd 10, sc in each of next 83 sc, **sc dec** *(see Stitch Guide)* in next 2 sts. Leaving rem 15 sc unworked, turn.

Rnd 13: Sc in each sc across to last 2 sc, sc dec in last 2 sc, turn.

Rnds 14–17: Rep rnd 13. At end of last rnd, fasten off orange-red.

Rnd 18: With 2 strands tan held tog, using H hook, sc in each sc, in end of each row and rem unworked sts of row 12. Fasten off.

DOG BLANKET
BODY

Row 1: With size H hook and fuchsia, ch 41, sc in 2nd ch from hook and each rem ch across, turn.

Row 2: Ch 2, hdc in each sc across, turn.

Row 3: Ch 3, dc in each hdc across, turn.

Row 4: Rep row 2.

Row 5: Ch 1, sc in each st across, turn.

Next rows: Changing colors *(see Stitch Guide)* to pale green, coral or yellow as shown in photo or as desired, rep rows 2–5 consecutively until Blanket reaches designated size.

BORDER
With last color used, working in sts and in ends of rows around outside edge of Blanket, sc evenly sp around.

DOG TOY
Rnd 1: With size E hook and variegated yarn, ch 2, 7 sc in 2nd ch from hook, **do not join** *(see Pattern Notes)*, **mark beg of rnd** *(see Pattern Notes)*.

Rnd 2: 2 sc in each sc around. *(14 sc)*

Rnd 3: [2 sc in next sc, sc in next sc] around. *(21 sc)*

Rnds 4–8: Sc in each sc around.

Rnd 9: [**Sc dec** *(see Stitch Guide)* in next 2 sts, sc in next sc] around. *(14 sc)*

Rnd 10: [Sc dec in next 2 sts] around. *(7 sc)*

FINISHING
Safety note: If intended recipient is 4 years of age or younger, do not attach bells.

Cut yarn, leaving 8-inch tail. Weave tail through 7 sts, pull tight to close. Sew 1 jingle bell to each end of Toy. ∎

Afghan for Doll & Child

DESIGNS BY FRANCES HUGHES

SKILL LEVEL

INTERMEDIATE

FINISHED SIZES

Doll's Afghan: 18 x 22 inches
Child's Afghan: 28½ x 37 inches

MATERIALS

- Light (DK) weight yarn:
  7 oz/712 yds/200g white (MC)
  3½ oz/348 yds/100g each yellow
  (A), coral (B), aqua (C) and
  purple (D)
- Size F/5/3.75mm crochet hook
  or size needed to obtain gauge
- Tapestry needle
- Stitch markers

3
LIGHT

GAUGE

Motif = 4¼ x 4¼ inches

PATTERN NOTES

Weave in ends as work progresses.

Join with slip stitch as indicated unless otherwise
  stated.

Chain-3 at beginning of round counts as first
  double crochet unless otherwise stated.

SPECIAL STITCHES

Beginning V-stitch (beg V-st): Ch 4 *(counts as dc
and ch-1 sp)*, dc in same st as joining.

V-stitch (V-st): (Dc, ch 1, dc) in indicated st.

**Beginning 3-double crochet cluster (beg 3-dc
cl):** Ch 3, [yo, insert hook in same st or sp as
joining, draw up lp, yo, draw through 2 lps on
hook] twice, yo, draw through 3 lps on hook.

3-double crochet cluster (3-dc cl): [Yo, insert
hook in indicated st or sp, draw up lp, yo,
draw through 2 lps on hook] 3 times, yo, draw
through 4 lps on hook.

DOLL'S AFGHAN
MOTIF 1
MAKE 3.

Rnd 1 (RS): With A, ch 4, **join** *(see Pattern Notes)*
in first ch to form a ring, **ch 3** *(see Pattern
Notes)*, 15 dc in ring, join in 3rd ch of beg ch-3.
Fasten off. *(16 dc)*

Rnd 2: With RS facing, join B in any dc, **beg V-st**
(see Special Stitches), *ch 1, sk next dc, (**3-dc cl**—
see Special Stitches, ch 2, 3-dc cl) in next dc, ch 1,
sk next dc**, **V-st** *(see Special Stitches)* in next dc,
rep from * 3 times, ending last rep at **, join in
3rd ch of beg ch-4. Fasten off. *(4 V-sts, 8 3-dc cl,
4 corner ch-2 sps)*

Rnd 3: With RS facing, join C in any corner ch-2
sp, **beg 3-dc cl** *(see Special Stitches)*, ch 2, 3-dc cl
in same ch-sp as joining, *ch 1, dc in next ch-1
sp, ch 1, 3-dc cl in ch-sp of next V-st, ch 1, dc
in next ch-1 sp, ch 1**, (3-dc cl, ch 2, 3-dc cl) in
next corner ch-2 sp, rep from * 3 times, ending
last rep at **, join in top of beg 3-dc cl. Fasten
off. *(12 3-dc cl, 8 dc, 4 corner ch-2 sps)*

Rnd 4: With RS facing, join MC in any corner
ch-2 sp, ch 3, 4 dc in same ch-sp as joining, place
marker in 2nd dc of 4 dc made for corner, dc in
each rem st and ch-1 sp around, working 5 dc in
each corner ch-2 sp, place marker in 3rd dc of 5 dc
made for corner, join in 3rd ch of beg ch-3. *(56 dc)*

Rnd 5: Ch 1, sc in same ch as joining, sc in each
st around, moving markers to coordinating sts
to mark corner sts, join in first sc. Fasten off.
(56 sc)

MOTIF 2
MAKE 3.
Rnd 1: With B, rep rnd 1 of Motif 1.

Rnd 2: With C, rep rnd 2 of Motif 1.

Rnd 3: With D, rep rnd 3 of Motif 1.

Rnds 4 & 5: With MC, rep rnds 4 and 5 of Motif 1.

MOTIF 3
MAKE 3.
Rnd 1: With C, rep rnd 1 of Motif 1.

Rnd 2: With D, rep rnd 2 of Motif 1.

Rnd 3: With A, rep rnd 3 of Motif 1.

Rnds 4 & 5: With MC, rep rnds 4 and 5 of Motif 1.

MOTIF 4
MAKE 3.
Rnd 1: With D, rep rnd 1 of Motif 1.

Rnd 2: With A, rep rnd 2 of Motif 1.

Rnd 3: With B, rep rnd 3 of Motif 1.

Rnds 4 & 5: With MC, rep rnds 4 and 5 of Motif 1.

ASSEMBLY
Referring to Motif Placement Diagram *(see page 23)*, join Motifs tog in 4 rows of 3 Motifs each, between marked corner sts.

BORDER
Rnd 1: With RS facing, join MC in any marked corner st, ch 3, 2 dc in same st as joining, move marker to first dc worked to mark corner st, dc in each st around, working 3 dc in each of 3 rem marked corner sts, move markers to 2nd dc worked in each corner to mark corner sts, join in 3rd ch of beg ch-3. Fasten off.

Rnd 2: With A, rep rnd 1.

Rnd 3: With B, rep rnd 1.

Rnd 4: With D, rep rnd 1.

Rnd 5: With C, rep rnd 1. Do not fasten off.

Rnd 6: [Ch 5, sk next st, sc in next st] around. Fasten off.

CHILD'S AFGHAN
MOTIF 1
MAKE 9.
Rnd 1: With A, rep rnd 1 of Motif 1 of Doll's Afghan.

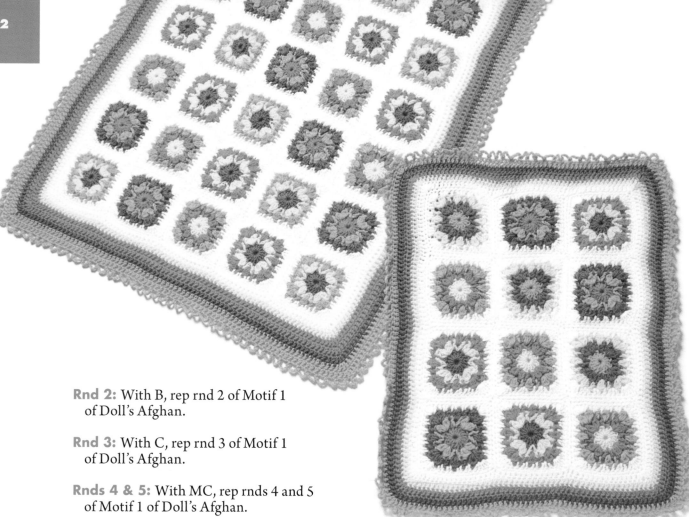

Rnd 2: With B, rep rnd 2 of Motif 1 of Doll's Afghan.

Rnd 3: With C, rep rnd 3 of Motif 1 of Doll's Afghan.

Rnds 4 & 5: With MC, rep rnds 4 and 5 of Motif 1 of Doll's Afghan.

MOTIF 2
MAKE 9.
Rnd 1: With B, rep rnd 1 of Motif 1 of Doll's Afghan.

Rnd 2: With C, rep rnd 2 of Motif 1 of Doll's Afghan.

Rnd 3: With D, rep rnd 3 of Motif 1 of Doll's Afghan.

Rnds 4 & 5: With MC, rep rnds 4 and 5 of Motif 1 of Doll's Afghan.

MOTIF 3
MAKE 9.
Rnd 1: With D, rep rnd 1 of Motif 1 of Doll's Afghan.

Rnd 2: With A, rep rnd 2 of Motif 1 of Doll's Afghan.

Rnd 3: With C, rep rnd 3 of Motif 1 of Doll's Afghan.

Rnds 4 & 5: With MC, rep rnds 4 and 5 of Motif 1 of Doll's Afghan.

MOTIF 4
MAKE 8.
Rnd 1: With D, rep rnd 1 of Motif 1 of Doll's Afghan.

Rnd 2: With A, rep rnd 2 of Motif 1 of Doll's Afghan.

Rnd 3: With B, rep rnd 3 of Motif 1 of Doll's Afghan.

Rnds 4 & 5: With MC, rep rnds 4 and 5 of Motif 1 of Doll's Afghan.

ASSEMBLY
Referring to Motif Placement Diagram *(see page 23)*, join Motifs tog in 7 rows of 5 Motifs each, between marked corner sts.

BORDER
Rnd 1: With RS facing, join MC in any marked corner st, ch 1, 3 sc in same st as joining, move marker to 2nd sc worked to mark corner st, sc in each st around, working 3 sc in each of 3 rem marked corner sts, move markers to 2nd sc worked in each corner to mark corner sts, join in first sc.

Rnd 2: Ch 3, 3 dc in next st, move marker to 2nd dc worked to mark corner st, dc in each st around, working 3 dc in each of 3 rem marked corner sts, move markers to 2nd dc worked in each corner to mark corner sts, join in 3rd ch of beg ch-3. Fasten off.

Rnd 3: With RS facing, join A in any marked corner st, ch 3, 2 dc in same st as joining, move marker to first dc worked to mark corner st, dc in each st around, working 3 dc in each of 3 rem marked corner sts, move markers to 2nd dc worked in each corner to mark corner st, join in 3rd ch of beg ch-3. Fasten off.

Rnd 4: With B, rep rnd 3. Do not fasten off.

Rnd 5: Rep rnd 2.

Rnd 6: With D, rep rnd 3.

Rnd 7: With C, rep rnd 3. **Do not fasten off.**

Rnd 8: Rep rnd 2. Do not fasten off.

Rnd 9: [Ch 5, sk next st, sc in next st] around. Fasten off. ∎

Child's Afghan
Motif Placement Diagram

Doll's Afghan
Motif Placement Diagram

COLOR KEY
1	Motif 1
2	Motif 2
3	Motif 3
4	Motif 4

Annie's Attic®

Dolly & Me Accessories & Toys is published by DRG, 306 East Parr Road, Berne, IN 46711. Printed in USA. Copyright © 2011 DRG. All rights reserved. This publication may not be reproduced in part or in whole without written permission from the publisher.

RETAIL STORES: If you would like to carry this pattern book or any other DRG publications, visit DRGwholesale.com.

Every effort has been made to ensure that the instructions in this publication are complete and accurate. We cannot, however, take responsibility for human error, typographical mistakes or variations in individual work. Please visit AnniesCustomerCare.com to check for pattern updates.

ISBN: 978-1-59635-395-4

123456789

STITCH GUIDE

STITCH ABBREVIATIONS

beg	begin/begins/beginning
bpdc	back post double crochet
bpsc	back post single crochet
bptr	back post treble crochet
CC	contrasting color
ch(s)	chain(s)
ch-	refers to chain or space previously made (i.e., ch-1 space)
ch sp(s)	chain space(s)
cl(s)	cluster(s)
cm	centimeter(s)
dc	double crochet (singular/plural)
dc dec	double crochet 2 or more stitches together, as indicated
dec	decrease/decreases/decreasing
dtr	double treble crochet
ext	extended
fpdc	front post double crochet
fpsc	front post single crochet
fptr	front post treble crochet
g	gram(s)
hdc	half double crochet
hdc dec	half double crochet 2 or more stitches together, as indicated
inc	increase/increases/increasing
lp(s)	loop(s)
MC	main color
mm	millimeter(s)
oz	ounce(s)
pc	popcorn(s)
rem	remain/remains/remaining
rep(s)	repeat(s)
rnd(s)	round(s)
RS	right side
sc	single crochet (singular/plural)
sc dec	single crochet 2 or more stitches together, as indicated
sk	skip/skipped/skipping
sl st(s)	slip stitch(es)
sp(s)	space(s)/spaced
st(s)	stitch(es)
tog	together
tr	treble crochet
trtr	triple treble
WS	wrong side
yd(s)	yard(s)
yo	yarn over

YARN CONVERSION

OUNCES TO GRAMS	GRAMS TO OUNCES
1 .... 28.4	25 .... ⅞
2 .... 56.7	40 .... 1⅔
3 .... 85.0	50 .... 1¾
4 .... 113.4	100 .... 3½

UNITED STATES		UNITED KINGDOM
sl st (slip stitch)	=	sc (single crochet)
sc (single crochet)	=	dc (double crochet)
hdc (half double crochet)	=	htr (half treble crochet)
dc (double crochet)	=	tr (treble crochet)
tr (treble crochet)	=	dtr (double treble crochet)
dtr (double treble crochet)	=	ttr (triple treble crochet)
skip	=	miss

Reverse single crochet (reverse sc): Ch 1, sk first st, working from left to right, insert hook in next st from front to back, draw up lp on hook, yo, and draw through both lps on hook.

Chain (ch): Yo, pull through lp on hook.

Single crochet (sc): Insert hook in st, yo, pull through st, yo, pull through both lps on hook.

Double crochet (dc): Yo, insert hook in st, yo, pull through st, [yo, pull through 2 lps] twice.

Front loop (front lp) Back loop (back lp)

Front Loop   Back Loop

Front post stitch (fp): Back post stitch (bp): When working post st, insert hook from right to left around post of st on previous row.

Back   Front

Post of Stitch

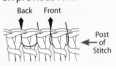

Half double crochet (hdc): Yo, insert hook in st, yo, pull through st, yo, pull through all 3 lps on hook.

Double treble crochet (dtr): Yo 3 times, insert hook in st, yo, pull through st, [yo, pull through 2 lps] 4 times.

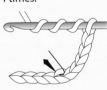

Slip stitch (sl st): Insert hook in st, pull through both lps on hook.

Chain color change (ch color change) Yo with new color, draw through last lp on hook.

Double crochet color change (dc color change) Drop first color, yo with new color, draw through last 2 lps of st.

Treble crochet (tr): Yo twice, insert hook in st, yo, pull through st, [yo, pull through 2 lps] 3 times.

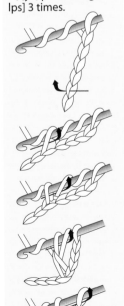

Single crochet decrease (sc dec): (Insert hook, yo, draw lp through) in each of the sts indicated, yo, draw through all lps on hook.

Half double crochet decrease (hdc dec): (Yo, insert hook, yo, draw lp through) in each of the sts indicated, yo, draw through all lps on hook.

Double crochet decrease (dc dec): (Yo, insert hook, yo, draw lp through, yo, draw through 2 lps on hook) in each of the sts indicated, yo, draw through all lps on hook.

Treble crochet decrease (tr dec): Holding back last lp of each st, tr in each of the sts indicated, yo, pull through all lps on hook.

Example of 2-sc dec   Example of 2-hdc dec

Example of 2-dc dec

Example of 2-tr dec

U.S. $8.95 CANADA $10.95

UPC

7 32526 40624 9

PRINTED IN USA
AnniesAttic.com

EAN

ISBN: 978-1-59635-395-4

5 0 8 9 5

9 781596 353954